Living as a Beloved Daughter of God

A Faith-Sharing Guide for Catholic Women

D0561730

Living as a Beloved Daughter of God

A Faith-Sharing Guide for Catholic Women

Patricia Mitchell and Bill Bawden

The Word Among Us Press
9639 Doctor Perry Road
Ijamsville, Maryland 21754
www.wordamongus.org

ISBN: 978-1-59325-052-2

Made and printed in the United States of America
11 10 09 08   4 5 6 7

Cover and Book Design: David Crosson

Imprimatur: +Most Reverend Eusebius J. Beltran
Archbishop of Oklahoma City
December 31, 2004

Scripture citations are taken from the New Revised Standard Version Bible: Catholic Edition, copyright ©1989, 1993, Division of Christian Education of the National Council of the Churches of Christ in the United States of America. Used by permission. All rights reserved.

Excerpts from the English translation of the *Catechism of the Catholic Church* for use in the United States of America, copyright © 1994, United States Catholic Conference, Inc.— Libreria Editrice Vaticana. Used with permission.

Library of Congress Cataloging-in-Publication Data
Mitchell, Patricia, 1953-
Living as a beloved daughter of God : a faith-sharing guide for Catholic women / Patricia Mitchell and Bill Bawden.
    p. cm.
ISBN 1-59325-052-5 (alk. paper)
1. Catholic women--Religious life. I. Bawden, Bill, 1938- II. Title.
BX2353.M58 2005
248.8'43'088282--dc22
                            2004030555

Contents

Acknowledgments

We are grateful to those women who took each one of these sessions to prayer and offered critiques and suggestions that were helpful in refining our ideas: Shellie Greiner, Pam Valvo, Angela Burrin, Theresa Difato, and Sr. Paula Hagen. We would also like to thank Margaret Procario for copyediting, Kay Janda and Carrie Smoot for proofreading, and David Crosson for design.

Introduction

I have called you by name, you are mine. (Isaiah 43:1)

A daughter gives such joy to her parents! She is a tangible reflection of their love, and they delight in her—not for what she does but for who she is. In the same way, God delights in you, for you are his beloved daughter. He has called you by name, and you belong to him.

You might not identify yourself, first and foremost, as a beloved daughter of God, and yet, by virtue of your baptism, that's who you are. Through his death and resurrection, Jesus reconciled us to his Father so that we could become adopted children of God (Colossians 1:19-20; Galatians 4:4-7). So how do we experience the reality of this awesome truth about ourselves and our relationship with God?

We hope this guide will help you answer that question and launch you on a Spirit-filled journey to a deeper and more rewarding faith life. From our own experience, we know that just taking the time to prayerfully reflect on topics such as those presented in *Living as a Beloved Daughter of God* will bring you into a closer relationship with your Father in heaven—and with your "sisters" in Christ with whom you share your faith.

Living as a Beloved Daughter of God was conceived and written after the enthusiastic reception of a similar guide for men, *Signposts: How To Be a Catholic Man in the World Today* (The Word Among Us Press, 1999). Coauthored by Deacon Bill Bawden, who is also a coauthor of this book, *Signposts* has been used by thousands of men in small fellowship groups in Catholic parishes across the country. The response to *Signposts* was so positive that soon many women—including wives of the men who participated in those fellowship groups—began to ask for a book that was specifically designed for them. Although the format of this book differs somewhat from *Signposts*, its goal is the same: to encourage Catholics of any age or situation in life to deepen their faith through prayer, reflection, and fellowship.

Both men and women who have attended small faith-sharing groups quickly discover the benefits they offer. Members support and affirm one another by sharing their insights about the challenges they face in their homes, work, and spiritual lives. In doing so, they cultivate lasting friendships with other parishioners, have fun, and learn from one another. They also come to a deeper understanding and appreciation of the richness and beauty of their Catholic faith. Even if you are not in a formal small group, you can benefit from using this study guide, either by yourself or with one or two friends.

Living as a Beloved Daughter of God is divided into two parts. The first eight sessions are designed to encourage you to grow closer to God through prayer, Scripture, and the sacraments. The second eight sessions will help you grow as a disciple of Christ. Each session begins with an introduction and a short story about a woman who is dealing with a specific aspect of her faith. A Scripture passage and several paragraphs from the *Catechism of the Catholic Church* have been selected to support the theme for that session. The questions provide a basis for personal reflection and group discussion.

Guidelines for Small Group Meetings
A strong facilitator is of great value in using this guide. She doesn't need to be an expert in Scripture or church doctrine, although a knowledge of both would be helpful. And she doesn't function as a teacher. Rather, she "guides" the group, by keeping everyone focused on the particular subject, seeing that each woman in the group has an opportunity to participate, and keeping the discussion moving along.

If the group is newly organized, we suggest that one person serve as facilitator. After the group has bonded and the women have become comfortable with one another, the facilitator's role may be rotated among the women who are interested in leading the discussion. This will prepare women to lead another group when the current one grows beyond eight or ten members.

Here are some guidelines that will help the members of your group get the most out of their time together:

Opening Prayer

A time of prayer to open your sessions will provide everyone with the opportunity to come into the presence of the Lord. The specific format is up to you. You might choose to begin with a traditional prayer, such as the Our Father or the Hail Mary, or even a decade of the rosary. Or, you could try spontaneous prayer from the group or a brief prayer service planned by one of the participants. You may also want to sing a hymn or play a CD.

Accountability

Preparing ahead for the sessions will ensure greater participation and more fruitful discussions. So it's important that all the women plan to devote some time before each meeting to reading the Scripture passages and *Catechism* references and answering the questions that follow. Scripture texts from the New Revised Standard Version are included in each chapter so that the members of the group can all refer to the same translation. Specific paragraphs from the *Catechism* are cited but only a portion is reprinted in the text, so it's helpful for the participants to have a copy of their own. The complete *Catechism* is also available on the Internet, for anyone who doesn't already own a copy.

Facilitators should encourage participants to attend as many meetings as possible. Not only does regular participation provide coherence and consistency to the group discussions, it also demonstrates that members value one another and are committed to sharing their lives with one another.

Confidentiality
Faith sharing can only be honest and personal if participants feel that they can completely trust one another. Facilitators should stress ahead of time that whatever is said at the meetings is strictly confidential. It's a good idea to remind the group of that point periodically, as well. Then, as the women in the group become more comfortable with one another, they will feel increasingly able to share their faith experiences on ever deeper levels.

Timing
Each session is designed to be covered in ninety minutes. Depending on the interaction of the group, how well the participants have prepared, or the amount of time spent in sharing and prayer, the time needed to cover the material in each session may vary. Nevertheless, since the participants have other commitments, it's important to try to start and stop on time. You might decide to skip some of the questions so that you still end on schedule. Or, if a particularly interesting discussion is underway, the group may choose to continue that session at the next meeting. Above all, try to be sensitive to the needs of the members of your group, since they are making a time commitment in order to participate.

Concluding Prayer
The meetings should always be closed with a prayer of thanksgiving. This would be a good time to pray for any of the women in the group who need God's grace.

Other Suggestions

■ Start with a few moments of socializing. You may want to offer drinks or snacks at the meeting.

■ Be flexible. While a predictable format is helpful, flexibility is also necessary at times to adjust to an individual's needs.

■ Encourage personal witnessing and testimonies to build faith.

■ Form teams of two women who will call each other during the week to encourage one another.

■ Be ready to welcome new members to the group, and to break up into two groups if the original group grows too large.

■ Space the sessions according to your group's needs. If the members of your group find it too difficult to meet for sixteen weeks consecutively, they can agree to meet for eight weeks and then begin sessions nine through sixteen at a later time. Or, you can meet biweekly or monthly—whatever works for your group.

As you journey through these sixteen sessions, may you experience God's love for you as his beloved daughter, and may this love inflame your heart so that you become a powerful witness to Christ and his church.

Patricia Mitchell   Deacon Bill Bawden

Part One

Beloved of the Father

Why Was 1 I Created?

$\mathcal{L}$ife is so busy! We are wives, mothers, sisters, grandmothers, employees, and parishioners. We can be so busy, in fact, and so intent on fulfilling our many and varied roles that we forget about our most important vocation: We are daughters of our Father in heaven! And because we are beloved daughters of God, we need to step back and ask God how he wants us to live—and wait to hear his answers.

Ann had always been goal oriented and focused on success. She became a lawyer and landed a plum job in a prestigious law firm. Ann worked long hours under lots of pressure for several years with the goal of making partner. The time and energy she expended at work gave her little time to spend with her parents, with friends, or in volunteer activities at her church. However, she told herself that once she made partner, she'd have plenty of time for all these things. Then, in one month's time, she was unexpectedly let go from the law firm and was diagnosed with a stress-related illness. Suddenly Ann found herself questioning all her past decisions. Had she been missing what was most important in life?

Ann met with her pastor, who urged her to spend some time in prayer. He suggested that she ask the Lord this question: Why did God create me, and what plan does he have for my life? As she prayed, Ann realized that for many years she had focused on shortsighted goals that were of her own making. God had created her to share in his own life. By virtue of her baptism, she was a beloved daughter of God. That was her deepest identity. She decided that everything in her life should flow first and foremost from that truth.

Scripture: Ephesians 1:3–14, 17–19

^{3}Blessed be the God and Father of our Lord Jesus Christ, who has blessed us in Christ with every spiritual blessing in the heavenly places, ^{4}just as he chose us in Christ before the foundation of the world to be holy and blameless before him in love. ^{5}He destined us for adoption as his children through Jesus Christ, according to the good pleasure of his will, ^{6}to the praise of his glorious grace that he freely bestowed on us in the Beloved. ^{7}In him we have redemption through his blood, the forgiveness of our trespasses, according to the riches of his grace ^{8}that he lavished on us. With all wisdom and insight ^{9}he has made known to us the mystery of his will, according to his good pleasure that he set forth in Christ, ^{10}as a plan for the fullness of time, to gather up all things in him, things in heaven and things on earth. ^{11}In Christ we have also obtained an inheritance, having been destined according to the purpose of him who accomplishes all things according to his counsel and will, ^{12}so that we, who were the first to set our hope on Christ, might live for the praise of his glory. ^{13}In him you also, when you had heard the word of truth, the gospel of your salvation, and had believed in him, were marked with the seal of the promised Holy Spirit; ^{14}this is the pledge of our inheritance toward redemption as God's own people, to the praise of his glory. . . .

^{17}I pray that the God of our Lord Jesus Christ, the Father of glory, may give you a spirit of wisdom and revelation as you come to know him, ^{18}so that, with the eyes of your heart enlightened, you may know what is the hope to which he has called you, what are the riches of his glorious inheritance among the saints, ^{19}and what is the immeasurable greatness of his power for us who believe, according to the working of his great power.

1. Why do you think God wanted us to become his daughters? How did Christ's death and resurrection make this possible?

_____

_____

_____

_____

_____

2. What do you think it means, in your life, to live for the praise of God's glory (1:12)?

_____

_____

_____

_____

_____

3. As a daughter of God, how can you know and experience "the hope to which you were called" (1:18)?

_____

_____

_____

_____

_____

Catechism: 1, 356–358

God, infinitely perfect and blessed in himself, in a plan of sheer good-ness freely created man to make him share in his own blessed life. For this reason, at every time and in every place, God draws close to man. (1)

Being in the image of God the human individual possesses the dig-nity of a person, who is not just something, but someone. He is capa-ble of self-knowledge, of self-possession and of freely giving himself and entering into communion with other persons. And he is called by grace to a covenant with his Creator, to offer him a response of faith and love that no other creature can give in his stead. (357)

1. Why do you think God created you, personally? How does this make you feel?

_____

_____

_____

_____

2. Share some concrete ways that you can share in God's own life.

_____

_____

_____

_____

_____

3. What has been your response at different times in your life to God's offer to enter into a covenant with him?

_____

_____

_____

_____

_____

For Further Reflection and Discussion:

1. Many women struggle with low self-esteem. On what do you currently base your self-worth? If you would like to see that change, how would a deeper awareness of God's love for you help?

_____

_____

_____

_____

_____

2. What are your distinctive qualities and gifts that show that God has created you for a unique purpose? How do these unique gifts provide you with the capacity to make a difference in your family and in your community?

_____

_____

_____

_____

_____

3. Think back to some of the major decisions you have made in your life. How many were made based on your identity as a beloved daughter of God? How many were made for other reasons?

_____

_____

_____

_____

_____

4. How do you want to be remembered by your family, friends, and community? Upon your death, what would you want your friends and family to say in your eulogy?

_____

_____

_____

_____

_____

Jesus, the Word Made Flesh

*I*f you grew up in a Christian family, you grew up hearing about Jesus. You heard about his parables and miracles, his death and resurrection. Yet, there is a difference between knowing *about* someone and *knowing* someone personally. You might know everything there is to know about your favorite celebrity, for instance. Yet how different your relationship would be if you had the chance to become that celebrity's best friend!

While Melanie was getting to know her new neighbor Linda, she was struck by how much Jesus was a part of Linda's life. When Linda mentioned that Jesus wanted her to spend more one-on-one time with her youngest daughter, or that he asked her to trust her son to make the right choices for himself, she sounded as if she had been talking to a friend! In fact, she seemed as eager to share her thoughts with him when she was happy as she did when she needed his help.

It was so natural for Linda to talk about what she had learned from the Lord in her prayer time that Melanie began to desire that same intimate relationship with God. When Melanie told Linda of her desire, Linda suggested that she reserve time each morning just for Jesus. Linda said that Jesus would always be there, waiting to hear from her!

We all have that same standing invitation from Jesus. Jesus is our brother; we have the same Father. In fact, he wants to become our very best friend. He wants us to commit our lives to him and to develop a deep and intimate relationship with him.

Scripture: John 15:4–14

⁴Abide in me as I abide in you. Just as the branch cannot bear fruit by itself unless it abides in the vine, neither can you unless you abide in me. ⁵I am the vine, you are the branches. Those who abide in me and I in them bear much fruit, because apart from me you can do nothing. ⁶Whoever does not abide in me is thrown away like a branch and withers; such branches are gathered, thrown into the fire, and burned. ⁷If you abide in me, and my words abide in you, ask for whatever you wish, and it will be done for you. ⁸My Father is glorified by this, that you bear much fruit and become my disciples. ⁹As the Father has loved me, so I have loved you; abide in my love. ¹⁰If you keep my commandments, you will abide in my love, just as I have kept my Father's commandments and abide in his love. ¹¹I have said these things to you so that my joy may be in you, and that your joy may be complete.

¹²"This is my commandment, that you love one another as I have loved you. ¹³No one has greater love than this, to lay down one's life for one's friends. ¹⁴You are my friends if you do what I command you."

1. How can you better rely on Christ for sustenance and life, just as a branch to a vine?

_____

_____

_____

_____

_____

2. Why do you think Jesus links his friendship with following his commandment to love one another?

_____

_____

_____

_____

_____

3. What does abiding in Christ's love mean to you? Think of a specific situation in the last week when abiding in Christ's love helped you to take the right action.

_____

_____

_____

_____

_____

Catechism: 457–460

The Word became flesh . . .

> *in order to save us by reconciling us with God. . . .* (457)
> *so that thus we might know God's love. . . .* (458)
> *to be our model of holiness. . . .* (459)
> to make us *"partakers of the divine nature."* (460)

1. What does Jesus' sacrifice on the cross say to you about how much your heavenly Father loves you?

_____

_____

_____

2. Reflecting on Jesus' life, in what ways is he your model for holiness?

_____

_____

_____

_____

_____

3. What does "partakers of the divine nature" mean to you? How does your faith allow you to share in God's divinity through Jesus? Share a time when you experienced God's life of grace working in you.

_____

_____

_____

_____

_____

For Further Reflection and Discussion:

1. Think of several strong friendships you have enjoyed in your life. What characterized those friendships? How can you bring those characteristics into your friendship with Jesus?

_____

_____

_____

_____

2. In what ways have you given your life—heart, soul, and mind—to Jesus? In what ways are you holding anything back from him? How would it help you, in an extended time of prayer, to consciously give your life to Jesus?

_____

_____

_____

_____

_____

3. What are one or two specific things you can do in the following weeks to strengthen your relationship with Jesus?

_____

_____

_____

_____

_____

4. Choose one of your favorite gospel scenes. Spend a few minutes imagining yourself as part of that scene and interacting with Jesus. Make special note of Jesus' body language and facial expressions, especially the way he looks at you. What does he say to you? What do you say to him?

_____

_____

_____

_____

Discovering God's Mercy

Our Father sent Jesus into the world to pay the price for our redemption. Jesus took all the sins of the world upon himself. He defeated sin once and for all—and yet, because of our wounded nature as human beings, we are still inclined to sin. This inclination often requires us to do battle within ourselves to defeat temptation. Fortunately, through our baptism we became adopted daughters of God and received the life of Christ's grace. We can cling to God in our struggles and experience victory. And when we fail, we can rely on God's unconditional love and mercy and on the Sacrament of Reconciliation to bring us back to him.

Sometimes we don't realize how much we need to fight the temptation to sin until we find ourselves in grave sin. Donna had always been a practicing Catholic. However, at the age of twenty-eight, she found herself unhappy in her marriage, began to flirt with a coworker, and started having an affair. The affair ended quickly, but the pain it caused her husband made Donna realize how very much she loved him and how her actions had nearly destroyed their marriage.

After a long and difficult process, Donna's husband was able to forgive her. His mercy allowed her to see the great and unconditional love and mercy of God. When Donna sought God's forgiveness in the Sacrament of Reconciliation, she opened herself to the Lord's healing presence. Over time, she was able to forgive herself, as well.

Scripture: Romans 5:6–9; 6:6–12

[6]For while we were still weak, at the right time Christ died for the ungodly. [7]Indeed, rarely will anyone die for a righteous person—though perhaps for a good person someone might actually dare to die. [8]But God proves his love for us in that while we still were sinners Christ died for us. [9]Much more surely then, now that we have been justified by his blood, will we be saved through him from the wrath of God. . . .

[6]We know that our old self was crucified with him so that the body of sin might be destroyed, and we might no longer be enslaved to sin. [7]For whoever has died is freed from sin. [8]But if we have died with Christ, we believe that we will also live with him. [9]We know that Christ, being raised from the dead, will never die again; death no longer has dominion over him. [10]The death he died, he died to sin, once for all; but the life he lives, he lives to God. [11]So you also must consider yourselves dead to sin and alive to God in Christ Jesus.

[12]Therefore, do not let sin exercise dominion in your mortal bodies, to make you obey their passions.

1. Scripture says that Jesus died for us even while we were still sinners (5:8). What does this say about God's unconditional love for us?

_____

_____

_____

_____

_____

2. What do you think St. Paul means when he says "our old self was crucified" with Jesus (6:6)? Share a time in your life when you were freed from a particular sin or pattern of sin and experienced victory in Christ.

_____

_____

_____

_____

_____

3. In what ways does being "alive to God in Christ Jesus" (6:11) help you to face daily trials and tribulations?

_____

_____

_____

_____

_____

Catechism: 402–409

Original sin . . . is a deprivation of original holiness and justice, but human nature has not been totally corrupted: it is wounded in the natural powers proper to it; subject to ignorance, suffering, and the dominion of death; and inclined to sin. . . . Baptism, by imparting the life of Christ's grace, erases original sin and turns a man back toward God, but the consequences for nature, weakened and inclined to evil, persist in man and summon him to spiritual battle. (405)

1. Why do you think it is important to recognize that even baptized Christians are inclined to sin?

_____

_____

_____

_____

_____

2. Our weakened nature requires us to do spiritual battle. What kind of spiritual disciplines do you think help us to win our daily battles with temptation and sin?

_____

_____

_____

_____

_____

3. In our journey to grow closer to the Lord, we must turn daily to Christ's redemptive love. How do you see this process of ongoing conversion unfolding in your life?

_____

_____

_____

_____

_____

For Further Reflection and Discussion:

1. Have you ever been faced with a strong temptation in your life, as Donna was? How did you deal with it? What could Donna have done to defeat the temptation before she succumbed to it?

_____

_____

_____

_____

_____

2. Have you known someone who felt that they had committed such a grievous sin that God could not forgive them? How would you counsel them?

_____

_____

_____

_____

_____

3. The church provides the Sacrament of Reconciliation for the forgiveness and absolution of sins. What fruits does this sacrament bear in your life?

_____

_____

_____

_____

_____

4. What dispositions of the heart are necessary to experience daily conversion? What part does grace play?

_____

_____

_____

_____

_____

Why Should I Pray?

4

When we think and talk about prayer, it's easy to get caught up in the externals: When should I pray? Where should I pray? How should I pray? These are all important questions, but the most important one to consider is this: Why should I pray?

Kim was part of a Bible study group and was struggling to answer that question herself. She prayed here and there, offering up a word of thanks or asking for help in a tough situation. However, prayer was not a foundational part of her life. But as she heard the other women discussing prayer, she realized that they did not view prayer as a duty. These women looked forward each day to spending time with their heavenly Father and listening to what he might say to them.

When asked the question "Why do I pray?" Monsignor Bruno Forte, rector of the Pontifical University of Theology in southern Italy, answered in this way:

> You ask me: Why pray? And I reply: to live. Yes, really to live, you have to pray. Why? Because to live is to love: a life without love is not a life. It is empty loneliness, a sad person. Only someone who loves is truly alive; and we only love when we are loved, when we are touched and transformed by love. . . . Now love is born from encounter and it finds life in encountering the love of God. . . . When we pray, we let God love us, and we are born into love, ever anew. Thus it is that when we pray we live, in time and in eternity. (*World Mission Magazine,* July 2003)

Scripture: Psalm 63:1–8

[1]O God, you are my God, I seek you,
    my soul thirsts for you;
my flesh faints for you,
    as in a dry and weary land
        where there is no water.
[2]So I have looked upon you in the sanctuary,
    beholding your power and glory.
[3]Because your steadfast love is better than life,
    my lips will praise you.
[4]So I will bless you as long as I live;
    I will lift up my hands and call on your name.

[5]My soul is satisfied as with a rich feast,
    and my mouth praises you with joyful lips
[6]when I think of you on my bed,
    and meditate on you in the watches of the night;
[7]for you have been my help,
    and in the shadow of your wings I sing for joy.
[8]My soul clings to you;
    your right hand upholds me.

1. Why do you think the psalmist is thirsting for God? When have you ever found yourself thirsting for God in a similar way?

_____

_____

_____

_____

_____

2. How is praise a response to God's love and goodness? How do you praise God in your prayer? How can worshipful music help you?

_____

_____

_____

_____

_____

3. In 63:8, how does the psalmist sees himself in relation to God? How do you see the Lord upholding you and your loved ones?

_____

_____

_____

_____

_____

Catechism: 2559–2565

The wonder of prayer is revealed beside the well where we come seeking water: there, Christ comes to meet every human being. It is he who first seeks us and asks us for a drink. Jesus thirsts; his asking arises from the depths of God's desire for us. Whether we realize it or not, prayer is the encounter of God's thirst with ours. God thirsts that we may thirst for him. (2560)

1. How does your own concept of prayer compare to the concepts presented in the *Catechism*? How often do you experience God seeking your attention? Your love?

_____

_____

_____

_____

2. Think about a time when your husband or someone you loved missed you and desired your presence. How would your prayer be different if you imagined that God desired your presence?

_____

_____

_____

_____

3. Why do you think the *Catechism* states that humility is the foundation of prayer (2559)? How does a humble heart make us more open to receiving what God has for us?

_____

_____

_____

_____

For Further Reflection and Discussion:

1. Many women find it difficult to carve out time for prayer because they are juggling the demands of work and family. For others, it may be hard to find a quiet place to pray. What obstacles do you encounter in trying to set aside a time to pray each day? How can you overcome them?

_____

_____

_____

_____

_____

2. Share how you pray each day. What has been the fruit of prayer in your life? In what ways has this deepened your relationship with the Lord?

_____

_____

_____

_____

_____

3. Do you ever find your time of prayer dry? What do you think causes this? Share ways you have discovered to enliven your prayer.

_____

_____

_____

_____

_____

4. Describe a time when the Lord spoke to you in prayer, perhaps through a Scripture passage, or a thought that popped into your mind unexpectedly that you knew couldn't come from you. What helps you to listen to God as you pray?

_____

_____

_____

_____

_____

Hearing God in Scripture

If you knew that someone had written you a love letter, wouldn't you be eager to read it? That's what Scripture is: a love letter from your Father in heaven to you, his beloved daughter. In the Bible, God not only tells us how much he loves us, he also reveals himself to us.

Phyllis had always enjoyed hearing the Scriptures read at Mass, but she rarely opened up the Bible on her own. Then she was invited to join a neighborhood Bible study. Phyllis was surprised and amazed at how the Scriptures came alive as the women discussed them together. As she delved into Scripture more deeply, she began to realize what a rich treasure she had in God's word. Even when her Bible study group was not meeting, Phyllis tried to spend time each day reading Scripture.

One day, Phyllis' husband was rushed to the hospital with a heart attack. As the doctors wheeled him into the operating room for emergency bypass surgery, Phyllis prayed. As she did so, she saw herself in the small boat in the Sea of Galilee with Jesus during the violent storm (Matthew 8:23–27). She knew that even if Jesus was sleeping, he was in control. As she recalled the passage, Phyllis felt a great peace come over her. Later, as her husband was recuperating, Phyllis looked back on the situation and knew that the Lord had used Scripture to speak to her personally in a time of crisis.

Scripture: 2 Timothy 3:14–17

[14]But as for you, continue in what you have learned and firmly believed, knowing from whom you learned it, [15]and how from childhood you have known the sacred writings that are able to instruct you for salvation through faith in Christ Jesus. [16]All scripture is inspired by God and is useful for teaching, for reproof, for correction, and for training in righteousness, [17]so that everyone who belongs to God may be proficient, equipped for every good work.

1. St. Paul says that all Scripture is inspired by God. What difference does this make as you read and reflect on Scripture?

_____

_____

_____

_____

2. According to St. Paul, what role does Scripture play in growing as a disciple of Christ? What role has it played in your growth as a Christian?

_____

_____

_____

_____

3. In what ways can Scripture "equip" you for the work you do each day at home, in the office, or in your parish?

_____

_____

_____

_____

_____

Catechism: 101–108

In Sacred Scripture, the Church constantly finds her nourishment and her strength, for she welcomes it not as a human word, "but as what it really is, the word of God" (1 Thessalonians 2:13). "In the sacred books, the Father who is in heaven comes lovingly to meet his children, and talks with them" (*Dei Verbum*, 21). (104)

Christianity is the religion of the "Word" of God, "a word which is not a written and mute word, but the Word which is incarnate and living." If the Scriptures are not to remain a dead letter, Christ, the eternal Word of the living God, must, through the Holy Spirit, "open [our] minds to understand the Scriptures" (Luke 24:45). (108)

1. How often have you viewed Scripture as a way for the Father to talk to you, his beloved daughter? How does this knowledge increase your desire to spend time reading and praying with Scripture? How would keeping a prayer journal help you?

_____

_____

_____

_____

_____

2. What role does the Holy Spirit play as we read and reflect on Scripture? What role does the church play in ensuring that we don't misinterpret Scripture?

_____

_____

_____

_____

_____

3. What practical steps could you take to "open your mind" to better understand the Scriptures?

_____

_____

_____

_____

For Further Reflection and Discussion:

1. Share a challenging situation that you are experiencing in your life, whether it is a financial or health problem or a problem with an important relationship. What story from the Bible could help you better deal with this problem? What would Jesus say to you?

_____

_____

_____

_____

2. Who is your favorite woman in Scripture? Why?

_____

_____

_____

_____

_____

3. Jesus quoted the Scriptures on numerous occasions, including when he was dying on the cross. What would be the benefits to you of having Scripture inscribed on your heart as Jesus did?

_____

_____

_____

_____

4. If you have ever been involved in a Bible study, whether individually or in a group, what fruit did it bear in your life?

_____

_____

_____

_____

Encountering Christ in the Eucharist

Before he ascended to his Father, Jesus promised that he would be with us always (Matthew 28:20). And true to his promise, he remains with us always, in the Eucharist, where he is present body, blood, soul, and divinity. Pope John Paul II, in his encyclical *Dominicae Cenae*, notes that Jesus "awaits us in this sacrament of love" (3). Jesus' presence under the guise of ordinary bread and wine is a mystery that we grasp only by faith. Yet, when we come with faith and open hearts before the Blessed Sacrament, Jesus has so much to give us.

Jane and her husband were going through a difficult time. Their teenage son's rebellious attitudes and actions were affecting everyone in the family. They had tried a host of strategies to help him, but nothing was working. A friend suggested that they go to their parish's holy hour on Thursday nights and pray before the Blessed Sacrament. As they prayed together, they felt a strong sense of peace. They knew that the Lord wanted them to entrust their son to him. They left the church that night thankful for Christ's presence in the Eucharist.

Scripture: John 6: 51–58

[51]"I am the living bread that came down from heaven. Whoever eats of this bread will live forever; and the bread that I will give for the life of the world is my flesh."

[52]The Jews then disputed among themselves, saying, "How can this man give us his flesh to eat?" [53]So Jesus said to them, "Very truly, I tell you, unless you eat the flesh of the Son of Man and drink his blood, you have no life in you. [54]Those who eat my flesh and drink my blood have eternal life, and I will raise them up on the last day; [55]for my flesh is true food and my blood is true drink. [56]Those who eat my flesh and drink my blood abide in me, and I in them. [57]Just as the living Father sent me, and I live because of the Father, so whoever eats me will live because of me. [58]This is the bread that came down from heaven, not like that which your ancestors ate, and they died. But the one who eats this bread will live forever."

1. Jesus said, "Those who eat my flesh and drink my blood abide in me, and I in them" (6:56). Why do you think Jesus left us with the gift of his body and blood? What difference has this made to you personally in your faith journey?

_____

_____

_____

_____

_____

2. Why do you think Jesus called his body "true food" and his blood "true drink"? How does this food differ from the manna that sustained the Hebrews in the desert?

_____

_____

_____

_____

_____

3. Many disciples found Jesus' words to be a stumbling block and left him (John 6:60). Has belief in the real presence of the Eucharist ever been a stumbling block for you? If so, how did you or how are you resolving it?

_____

_____

_____

_____

_____

Catechism: 1373–1381

It is highly fitting that Christ should have wanted to remain present to his church in this unique way. Since Christ was about to take his departure from his own in his visible form, he wanted to give us his sacramental presence; since he was about to offer himself on the cross to save us, he wanted us to have the memorial of the love with which he loved us "to the end" (John 13:1), even to the giving of his life. In his Eucharistic presence he remains mysteriously in our midst as the one who loved us and gave himself up for us. . . . (1380)

1. Christ is present to us in many ways—in his word, in prayer, and in the poor and needy. How is Christ's presence in the Eucharist different from these other ways in which he manifests himself to us?

_____

_____

_____

_____

_____

2. Since Christ is truly present in the Eucharist, how is this sacrament meant to transform us? Unify us?

_____

_____

_____

_____

_____

3. Jesus is waiting for you to receive him in the Eucharist. How can the knowledge of this reality help you to experience his presence more deeply each time you receive him at Mass?

_____

_____

_____

_____

_____

For Further Reflection and Discussion:

1. Share a situation in which Jesus in the Eucharist has ministered to you personally. Can you think of a current circumstance in which you could invite Jesus in the Eucharist to minister to you?

_____

_____

_____

_____

_____

2. The minutes before we arrive at Sunday Mass can be hectic. How can the different parts of the Mass prepare us to come into the presence of the Lord and receive Holy Communion? How can we pray after we receive Jesus?

_____

_____

_____

_____

_____

3. The Second Vatican Council called the Eucharist "the source and summit of the Christian life" (_Lumen Gentium_, 11). How can you make the Eucharist more central to your own life? To your marriage? To your family?

_____

_____

_____

_____

_____

4. What is the difference between spending time in adoration of the Blessed Sacrament and receiving Jesus in the Eucharist? What do you think would be the benefits of a "holy hour" before the Blessed Sacrament?

_____

_____

_____

_____

_____

Receive the 7 Holy Spirit

On the evening before his crucifixion, Jesus promised his disciples that he would send his Holy Spirit to them (John 16:7–15). On the day of Pentecost, the Lord poured out his Spirit upon the apostles (Acts 2:33–36). In baptism, we receive new life in Christ and become temples of the Holy Spirit. In the Sacrament of Confirmation, we share more completely in the mission of Christ and are sealed with the gift of the Holy Spirit. As we grow and mature as Christians, we can awaken even more fully to the Spirit's work in our lives and truly live out our vocation as beloved daughters of our Father.

Even in very specific situations, we can ask the Holy Spirit to exercise his gifts in us. Janet's parents were celebrating their fiftieth wedding anniversary. She wanted to honor them in a special way, and thought about writing a prayer for them that she could read at their party—one that would give thanks to God for their life of faith. Janet didn't know if she could write such a prayer, so she asked the Holy Spirit to help her. When she sat down at the computer, she composed just the right prayer, and when it was read at the party, it brought tears to many of the guests who were present. The prayer so perfectly reflected her parents' life that Janet thought of it as written by the Holy Spirit himself.

Scripture: Acts 19:1–7

[1]While Apollos was in Corinth, Paul passed through the interior regions and came to Ephesus, where he found some disciples. [2]He said to them, "Did you receive the Holy Spirit when you became believers?" They replied, "No, we have not even heard that there is a Holy Spirit." [3]Then he said, "Into what then were you baptized?" They answered, "Into John's baptism." [4]Paul said, "John baptized with the baptism of repentance, telling the people to believe in the one who was to come after him, that is, in Jesus." [5]On hearing this, they were baptized in the name of the Lord Jesus. [6]When Paul had laid his hands on them, the Holy Spirit came upon them, and they spoke in tongues and prophesied—[7]altogether there were about twelve of them.

1. Why does Paul distinguish between the baptism of John and the baptism of Jesus? What was it about John's baptism that made these disciples from Ephesus open to being baptized in the name of Jesus?

_____

_____

_____

_____

_____

2. Why do you think Paul first baptized these disciples and then prayed with them to receive the Holy Spirit? What is the link between these two actions?

_____

_____

_____

_____

3. In the passage above, how did the Holy Spirit manifest himself? Are you open to these manifestations in your own life?

_____

_____

_____

_____

_____

Catechism: 731–736

He, then, gives us the "pledge" or "first fruits" of our inheritance: the very life of the Holy Trinity, which is to love as "God [has] loved us" (1 John 4:11–12). This love . . . is the source of the new life in Christ, made possible because we have received "power" from the Holy Spirit (Acts 1:8). (735)

By this power of the Spirit, God's children can bear much fruit. He who has grafted us onto the true vine will make us bear "the fruit of the Spirit: . . . love, joy, peace, patience, kindness, goodness, faithfulness, gentleness, self-control" (Galatians 5:22–23). (736)

1. As daughters of God, why do we need to have the power of the Holy Spirit operating in our lives?

_____

_____

_____

_____

_____

2. Describe how you see the role of the Holy Spirit in building up the Body of Christ and strengthening your relationships.

_____

_____

_____

_____

_____

3. Which gifts and fruits of the Spirit do you see manifested in your life (1 Corinthians 12:4–11 and Galatians 5:22–23)? Which of these gifts and fruits would you like to see grow more deeply in you?

_____

_____

_____

_____

_____

For Further Reflection and Discussion:

1. Share one event in your life in which you sensed or experienced the presence and power of the Holy Spirit.

_____

_____

_____

_____

_____

2. Many saints manifested the power of the Holy Spirit in their lives. Talk about one saint who has especially inspired you.

_____

_____

_____

_____

_____

3. The Holy Spirit is sometimes described in terms of fire because he can enkindle in us a more passionate love for God and for others. How do you think God uses passion and zeal in the lives of his disciples to accomplish his purposes? How do you think he wants to use your passion and zeal?

_____

_____

_____

_____

_____

4. If you have ever prayed for the Holy Spirit to come into your life in a more powerful way, describe what happened. How do you think praying in expectant faith for a greater outpouring of the Holy Spirit would change your life?

_____

_____

_____

_____

_____

The People of God, the Church

God wants to save us, not as lone individuals but as members of one another in him, through his church. The good news of Jesus Christ, preached by the apostles, has been handed down through the generations to us and safeguarded by the church. In baptism, we became beloved daughters of our Father and became part of one family, the People of God.

Because we live in an individualistic society, we can fall prey to a "God and me" spirituality, which can downplay the fact that we are members of a body of believers united in Christ. Our tendency toward individualism may also make it difficult for us to accept some of the church's teachings, especially on controversial issues. Under the inspiration of the Holy Spirit, the church is given the task of authentically interpreting and transmitting what God has revealed—and is revealing—to his people.

It often takes effort on our own part to study and understand the church's teachings. Julie and her husband Bill were struggling with infertility. They had been married for four years and desperately wanted children. As they researched their medical options, they discovered that the church considered some forms of infertility treatment immoral. At first they struggled to understand the church's reasoning, but as they studied it, they began to better appreciate its position. After praying about the issue, they decided to adopt children, and were overjoyed a year later when they welcomed a three-month-old infant from Korea into their home. Julie and Bill realized that the church's teaching was a source of wisdom, which had helped them to treasure the gift of human life in an increasingly confusing world.

Scripture: Matthew 16:13–19

[13]Now when Jesus came into the district of Caesarea Philippi, he asked his disciples, "Who do people say that the Son of Man is?" [14]And they said, "Some say John the Baptist, but others Elijah, and still others Jeremiah or one of the prophets." [15]He said to them, "But who do you say that I am?" [16]Simon Peter answered, "You are the Messiah, the Son of the living God." [17]And Jesus answered him, "Blessed are you, Simon son of Jonah! For flesh and blood has not revealed this to you, but my Father in heaven. [18]And I tell you, you are Peter, and on this rock I will build my church, and the gates of Hades will not prevail against it. [19]I will give you the keys of the kingdom of heaven, and whatever you bind on earth will be bound in heaven, and whatever you loose on earth will be loosed in heaven."

1. Jesus told Peter that his knowledge that he was the Son of the living God was revealed to him by his Father in heaven. Why was it necessary for Peter to experience this divine revelation about Jesus?

_____

_____

_____

_____

2. In the Acts of the Apostles, we see how Peter was a "rock" in the spreading of the gospel and the building of the early church. What can you do to be a bedrock of faith in your family and faith community?

_____

_____

_____

3. To Jews of Jesus' time, "binding" and "loosing" meant "allowing" and "forbidding." Why do you think Jesus wanted to give that authority to Peter?

_____

_____

_____

_____

Catechism: 96–100

What Christ entrusted to the apostles, they in turn handed on by their preaching and writing, under the inspiration of the Holy Spirit, to all generations, until Christ returns in glory. (96)

1. Despite their human failings, Jesus entrusted his apostles and those who followed them with the task of preaching and handing on the faith. Why do you think Jesus was able to trust human beings with so great a task?

_____

_____

_____

_____

2. Why is it crucial that our faith be safeguarded and handed down from generation to generation intact?

_____

_____

_____

_____

_____

3. What role do you play in handing on the faith to the next generation? Share some concrete ways that you have been able to transmit your faith to your children or to others in the next generation.

_____

_____

_____

_____

_____

For Further Reflection and Discussion:

1. What people and events in your life have shaped your ideas of what it means to be a member of the body of Christ? What has shaped your ideas about spiritual leadership and authority?

_____

_____

_____

_____

_____

2. What do you think would help to counter the tendency to adopt a "God and me" spirituality?

_____

_____

_____

_____

_____

3. Which attitudes of the heart helped Julie and Bill come to their decision? If there are church teachings that challenge or puzzle you, how could adopting those attitudes help you?

_____

_____

_____

_____

_____

4. What are some obstacles that young people face in our culture that prevent them from fully committing their lives to Christ? What could you do to make your parish more attractive to young people?

_____

_____

_____

_____

_____

Part Two

Living as a Daughter of God

Forgiveness and Reconciliation

As daughters of God, we need to have our Father's heart, a heart brimming over with mercy. Our Father is always ready to forgive us, and he asks that we forgive others as he forgives us. In each one of our relationships, whether it is with our husband, our parents, our children, our siblings, or our friends, we need to have this willingness to ask for and receive forgiveness. When mercy is lacking, our relationships cannot grow and thrive.

Lynda and Tammy are sisters who had been close to each other growing up. Even after they married, started families, and moved away from each other, they stayed in touch by calling each other every week. During one phone conversation, Lynda made a negative comment about Tammy's husband that deeply hurt Tammy. Lynda thought Tammy was being too sensitive, and Tammy thought Lynda shouldn't have been so thoughtless and critical. Both wanted the other to apologize first. For almost a year, the two sisters didn't communicate with each other.

One day at Mass, after hearing the Scripture passage about the prodigal son, Lynda felt an overwhelming sadness about the incident. She called Tammy on the phone and asked for her forgiveness. Tammy was reluctant at first to forgive her sister. Then she remembered how much she had missed their weekly phone conversations. "I forgive you," she told Lynda. Months later, the two sisters made a commitment to work out any future disagreements by immediately asking for and receiving forgiveness. Both regretted the year they had wasted.

Scripture: Matthew 18:21–35

[21]Then Peter came and said to him, "Lord, if another member of the church sins against me, how often should I forgive? As many as seven times?" [22]Jesus said to him, "Not seven times, but, I tell you, seventy-seven times.

[23]"For this reason the kingdom of heaven may be compared to a king who wished to settle accounts with his slaves. [24]When he began the reckoning, one who owed him ten thousand talents was brought to him; [25]and, as he could not pay, his lord ordered him to be sold, together with his wife and children and all his possessions, and payment to be made. [26]So the slave fell on his knees before him, saying, 'Have patience with me, and I will pay you everything.' [27]And out of pity for him, the lord of that slave released him and forgave him the debt. [28]But that same slave, as he went out, came upon one of his fellow slaves who owed him a hundred denarii; and seizing him by the throat, he said, 'Pay what you owe.' [29]Then his fellow slave fell down and pleaded with him, 'Have patience with me, and I will pay you.' [30]But he refused; then he went and threw him into prison until he would pay the debt. [31]When his fellow slaves saw what had happened, they were greatly distressed, and they went and reported to their lord all that had taken place. [32]Then his lord summoned him and said to him, 'You wicked slave! I forgave you all that debt because you pleaded with me. [33]Should you not have had mercy on your fellow slave, as I had mercy on you?' [34]And in anger his lord handed him over to be tortured until he would pay his entire debt. [35]So my heavenly Father will also do to every one of you, if you do not forgive your brother or sister from your heart."

1. What does this parable say about divine mercy? How would an awareness of our own sin help us to become more forgiving?

_____

_____

_____

_____

2. The difference in value between ten thousand talents and one hundred denarii was staggering. Why do you think Jesus used these numerical amounts in his parable?

_____

_____

_____

_____

3. What does it mean to forgive someone from the heart? What does Jesus say is the price for not forgiving?

_____

_____

_____

_____

Catechism: 2843–2844

It is not in our power not to feel or to forget an offense; but the heart that offers itself to the Holy Spirit turns injury into compassion and purifies the memory in transforming the hurt into intercession. (2843)

Forgiveness is a high-point of Christian prayer; only hearts attuned to God's compassion can receive the gift of prayer. Forgiveness also bears witness that, in our world, love is stronger than sin. (2844)

1. Why is forgiving another person often so difficult? What wrongful attitudes can get in the way?

_____

_____

_____

_____

_____

2. What are some practical ways we can attune our hearts to God's compassion so that we become more forgiving?

_____

_____

_____

_____

_____

3. How are love and forgiveness related? Think about a situation you witnessed personally or heard about that showed that "love is stronger than sin."

_____

_____

_____

_____

_____

_____

For Further Reflection and Discussion:

1. Why is it so important to ask for and receive forgiveness in our relationships? What happens if we fail to do so?

_____

_____

_____

_____

_____

2. What can you do to become a more forgiving person? What can help you learn to accept forgiveness from God and others?

_____

_____

_____

_____

_____

3. Share a time when you found it difficult to forgive someone. How were you able to reach a point in which you could pray for that person and wish the best for him or her?

_____

_____

_____

_____

_____

4. Is there someone in your life with whom you need to reconcile? If so, ask the Lord to give you a heart that desires reconciliation, along with the courage to approach that person. Ask the other members of your group to pray with and for you.

_____

_____

_____

_____

_____

The Power 10 Our Words

Women are noted for their relational skills, and most love to chat—especially with each other! However, often we don't realize the power of our words. We can use language to love and encourage others or to hurt them. We can fall into the habit of gossiping or speaking negatively or critically. We can become chronic complainers. However, once we become aware of how God wants us to speak to one another, we can replace destructive speech patterns with upbuilding ones. And when we fail—which we will inevitably do—we can ask others to forgive us!

When Lacey joined a Bible study group at her parish, she was immediately struck by how these women spoke to one another. They didn't complain about what their husbands or kids had done the previous week, like Lacey and her friends usually did when they got together. One woman was struggling in her relationship with her mother and asked for prayers, but didn't say anything critical about her. Another woman was facing a financial crisis, but she didn't complain or speak bitterly about the situation. Lacey loved the way the other women encouraged her when she told them about her doubts about being a good mother. Their words gave her confidence and inspired her to keep trying.

The group had pledged to keep confidential whatever was said at the Bible study. Lacey was skeptical at first, wondering if she could trust this agreement. But as others in the group felt safe sharing on a deeper, more personal level, so did Lacey. After several months of these weekly meetings, Lacey became convinced that she needed to change the way she spoke to people. She decided that she needed to find positive ways of conversing and relating with everyone, not just the women in her Bible study.

Scripture: James 3:2–10

[2]Anyone who makes no mistakes in speaking is perfect, able to keep the whole body in check with a bridle. [3]If we put bits into the mouths of horses to make them obey us, we guide their whole bodies. [4]Or look at ships: though they are so large that it takes strong winds to drive them, yet they are guided by a very small rudder wherever the will of the pilot directs. [5]So also the tongue is a small member, yet it boasts of great exploits.

How great a forest is set ablaze by a small fire! [6]And the tongue is a fire. The tongue is placed among our members as a world of iniquity; it stains the whole body, sets on fire the cycle of nature, and is itself set on fire by hell. [7]For every species of beast and bird, of reptile and sea creature, can be tamed and has been tamed by the human species, [8]but no one can tame the tongue—a restless evil, full of deadly poison. [9]With it we bless the Lord and Father, and with it we curse those who are made in the likeness of God. [10]From the same mouth come blessing and cursing. My brothers and sisters, this ought not to be so.

1. Why do you think James believed that if we control our tongues, we control our whole bodies? Based on your own experience, do you agree or disagree?

_____

_____

_____

_____

_____

2. What are some ways our speech can exert such power, both positive and negative?

_____

_____

_____

_____

_____

3. What have you found helpful in controlling your own tongue?

_____

_____

_____

_____

Catechism: 2477–2479

Detraction and calumny destroy the reputation *and honor of one's neighbor.* Honor is the social witness given to human dignity, and everyone enjoys a natural right to the honor of his name and reputation and to respect. Thus, detraction and calumny offend against the virtues of justice and charity. (2479)

1. Why is it wrong to be critical of someone, especially in front of a third person? When someone has a "critical spirit," what does that say about the state of that person's heart?

_____

_____

_____

_____

_____

2. What does it mean to you to "honor" someone? What are some ways you can honor your husband, children, or other family members?

_____

_____

_____

_____

3. According to the *Catechism*, we are guilty of detraction when, without an objectively valid reason, we disclose "another's faults and failings to persons who did not know them" (2477). Why do you think we are sometimes tempted to talk in this way?

_____

_____

_____

_____

_____

For Further Reflection and Discussion:

1. Think about your conversations over the past week. If you could change one or two things that you said, what would they be?

_____

_____

_____

_____

_____

2. When someone shares something personal with you, how often do you automatically assume that it is confidential? How can breaches of confidentiality destroy relationships?

_____

_____

_____

_____

_____

3. Share an experience when someone encouraged you when you were feeling dejected or inadequate. Why was it so important to hear those words? How is encouraging one another a way to build up the body of Christ?

_____

_____

_____

_____

_____

4. How can an awareness of your own failings help you to have a less critical spirit?

_____

_____

_____

_____

_____

Dealing with Our Emotions

Our emotions are gifts from God. Who could imagine being fully human without them? Yet we tend to lump emotions into two categories: "good" emotions, like affection and joy; and "bad" emotions, like anger and fear. In fact, in and of themselves emotions are neither good nor bad—it all depends on how we use and express them. We all know that emotions can get us into trouble, but they can also be the impetus for great acts of kindness and love. Because we are adopted daughters of our Father and a new creation in Christ, we should have confidence that we can express our emotions appropriately—without denying or suppressing them, or letting them get out of control.

Suzanne and her family were having breakfast when her five-year-old son spilled his orange juice on the floor. Suzanne jumped up from the table, scolded her son, and turned to her husband and said, "He's sitting next to you. Why didn't you stop him? Do I have to do everything around this house?"

In her prayer time later that morning, Suzanne was reflecting on the incident and realized she had flown off the handle about a relatively minor incident that didn't warrant the response she had given. The spill was an accident, and while she wished her son would be more careful, Suzanne knew that yelling at him probably wasn't going to keep him from spilling any more juice. And there was probably nothing that her husband could have done to prevent it, either. As she thought about the situation, she realized that her emotional outburst wasn't about the spilled orange juice or her husband's lack of responsibility. It was about the anger she felt toward her best friend, with whom she'd had a serious argument the day before.

Scripture: Ephesians 4:22–27, 31–32

²²You were taught to put away your former way of life, your old self, corrupt and deluded by its lusts, ²³and to be renewed in the spirit of your minds, ²⁴and to clothe yourselves with the new self, created according to the likeness of God in true righteousness and holiness.

²⁵So then, putting away falsehood, let all of us speak the truth to our neighbors, for we are members of one another. ²⁶Be angry but do not sin; do not let the sun go down on your anger, ²⁷and do not make room for the devil. . . .

³¹Put away from you all bitterness and wrath and anger and wrangling and slander, together with all malice, ³²and be kind to one another, tenderhearted, forgiving one another, as God in Christ has forgiven you.

1. According to St. Paul, what happens to the "old self" when we are clothed with the "new self"? How does our faith in Christ and in his power to give us new life help us to "put away" the old self?

_____

_____

_____

_____

_____

2. Why do you think Paul mentions the renewal of our minds? What is the connection between our minds and our emotions?

_____

_____

_____

_____

3. When Paul says "be angry but do not sin," what important truths is he expressing about our God-given emotions? How can righteous anger be used to further God's kingdom?

_____

_____

_____

_____

Catechism: 1767–1770

In themselves passions are neither good nor evil. They are morally qualified only to the extent that they effectively engage reason and will. . . . It belongs to the perfection of the moral or human good that the passions be governed by reason. (1767)

Passions are morally good when they contribute to a good action, evil in the opposite case. . . . Emotions and feelings can be taken up into the *virtues* or perverted by the *vices*. (1768)

1. Why do you think God created us with emotions? How do you think he wants us to express them?

_____

_____

_____

_____

_____

2. Think of a recent situation in which your emotions "engaged" your reason and will. What was the result? Did you take the right action, based on the feelings you were experiencing?

_____

_____

_____

_____

_____

3. How often do you fail to fully recognize what you are actually feeling? Why do you think this is so? How often do you find that anger masks a deeper feeling, such as hurt?

_____

_____

_____

_____

For Further Reflection and Discussion:

1. What were the family rules you learned as a child about how to express emotions? How have they affected your behavior as an adult?

_____

_____

_____

_____

2. How can you avoid the extremes of losing control of your emotions, on the one hand, or denying or suppressing them on the other?

_____

_____

_____

_____

_____

3. Think of an instance in which you allowed your emotions to control your actions, without giving those actions any thought beforehand. What was the result? Were you able to avoid that same mistake the next time you faced the same situation?

_____

_____

_____

_____

4. Women often suffer from mood swings. How can the truth about a renewed mind help us not give in to extreme moods?

_____

_____

_____

_____

Forming Friendships in Christ

God never intended for us to walk our faith journey alone. Our Father wants us to have brothers and sisters in Christ who can support us and help us to grow closer to him. Women need the friendship of other women—friendships that are caring, supportive, and life-giving.

Liz and Beth met each other at a local park one sunny day as their toddlers were running around the playground. As they chatted, they realized that they had much in common. They had grown up in close-knit families in the same part of the country. They belonged to the same parish, and their children were close in age. They exchanged phone numbers and quickly became close friends. Liz discovered that Beth had a strong prayer life, and it encouraged her to seek a deeper relationship with the Lord in Scripture, in prayer, and at Mass.

The following year, when a high-risk pregnancy forced Liz to go on bed rest, Beth often watched her two young sons and brought her meals. Several years later, Beth discovered she had breast cancer, and Liz was there to serve her, often cheering her up just by her presence over a cup of tea. Through the ups and downs of daily life, Liz and Beth prayed together and shared their insights about God, their families, and every other imaginable topic. As their children grew older and Beth and Liz took jobs outside the home, they didn't see each other as often. Yet twenty years later, their strong friendship continues. They consider their bond to be as close as blood sisters, and refer to themselves as "sisters in the Lord."

Scripture: Luke 1:39–45, 56

³⁹In those days Mary set out and went with haste to a Judean town in the hill country, ⁴⁰where she entered the house of Zechariah and greeted Elizabeth. ⁴¹When Elizabeth heard Mary's greeting, the child leaped in her womb. And Elizabeth was filled with the Holy Spirit ⁴²and exclaimed with a loud cry, "Blessed are you among women, and blessed is the fruit of your womb. ⁴³And why has this happened to me, that the mother of my Lord comes to me? ⁴⁴For as soon as I heard the sound of your greeting, the child in my womb leaped for joy. ⁴⁵And blessed is she who believed that there would be a fulfillment of what was spoken to her by the Lord." . . .

⁵⁶And Mary remained with her about three months and then returned to her home.

1. Mary went "with haste" to visit her cousin Elizabeth. Why do you think Mary was so eager to see her?

_____

_____

_____

_____

2. How did Mary and Elizabeth affirm, support, and rejoice in the vocations that God had given to each of them? Why was this important to their friendship?

_____

_____

_____

_____

_____

3. Elizabeth was in her "sixth month" (Luke 1:36) of pregnancy, and Mary remained with her for three months (1:56), probably until after Elizabeth's son, John the Baptist, was born. How do you think this extended period of time with Elizabeth helped Mary prepare for the birth of her own special son?

_____

_____

_____

_____

Catechism: 1939, 2346–47

The principle of solidarity, also articulated in terms of "friendship" or "social charity," is a direct demand of human and Christian brotherhood. (1939)

Charity is the *form* of all the virtues. Under its influence, chastity appears as a school of the gift of the person. . . . Chastity is expressed notably in *friendship with one's neighbor*. Whether it develops between persons of the same or opposite sex, friendship represents a great good for all. It leads to spiritual communion. (2346–2347)

1. How is the "gift of the person" related to friendship? What happens when it is lacking?

_____

_____

_____

_____

2. Solidarity is defined as a "union of interests, purposes, and sympathies" among members of a group. Why is solidarity critical to Christian brotherhood and sisterhood? How is Jesus' life a model of solidarity?

_____

_____

_____

_____

_____

3. How does our recognition that we are one in Christ affect our friendships?

_____

_____

_____

_____

For Further Reflection and Discussion:

1. Why do you think women need friendships with other women? What is something a woman friend can give you that your husband, a brother, or a male friend would find difficult to give?

_____

_____

_____

_____

_____

2. Why is it important to make time for friendships in your life? In what ways could you be a better friend? If you are lonely, how could you develop a relationship with a "sister in the Lord"?

_____

_____

_____

_____

_____

3. Reflect upon the differences in the qualities of your friendships. Are some friendships more life-giving than others? How does a spiritual component in a friendship help it to deepen and grow?

_____

_____

_____

_____

_____

4. Think about someone in your parish or elsewhere whom you sense is in need of friendship. What practical things could you do to share God's love with that person?

_____

_____

_____

_____

_____

Freedom from Worry and Anxiety

13

*J*esus came to set us free—not only from sin but also from anything that prevents us from living out our vocation as beloved daughters of the Father. Worry and anxiety can be chronic problems for many women and real obstacles to growing closer to God and building his kingdom on earth. However, we need to recognize how anxiety operates in our lives. Sometimes it can creep in so stealthily that we don't consciously notice it until we start experiencing stress-related symptoms like chronic headaches. Then we need to consciously place our trust in the Lord and have absolute confidence that Jesus can give us the victory to replace worry and anxiety with his peace.

Michelle had a lot on her mind. Her mother, who lived in another state, was having health problems. Her teenage son was doing poorly in school, and her husband's job was in jeopardy. Her own office deadlines were looming. But Michelle didn't realize how much her anxiety was consuming her until she started having trouble falling asleep at night. The insomnia was sporadic, but was definitely affecting her ability to stay alert and cheerful.

One day Michelle had lunch with her close friend, Barbara. As Michelle started listing all the issues that were worrying her, she realized that it was her anxiety that was keeping her awake at night. Barbara was sympathetic and offered to pray with her right on the spot. She encouraged Michelle to keep close watch on her thought patterns. When Michelle slipped into a worry mode, Barbara told her, she should surrender the problem to the

Lord in her daily prayer time and at other times as well, trusting that he was in control of the situation. Then she should claim God's peace. Even in the midst of her trials, the Lord would refresh her.

Scripture: Philippians 4:4–7

[4]Rejoice in the Lord always; again I will say, Rejoice. [5]Let your gentleness be known to everyone. The Lord is near. [6]Do not worry about anything, but in everything by prayer and supplication with thanksgiving let your requests be made known to God.[7]And the peace of God, which surpasses all understanding, will guard your hearts and your minds in Christ Jesus.

1. What is St. Paul's antidote to worry and anxiety?

_____

_____

_____

_____

2. How can God's peace "surpass all understanding"(4:7)? Have you ever experienced such peace? What was it like?

_____

_____

_____

_____

3. Why do you think St. Paul mentions thanksgiving when making requests to God? How can a grateful attitude help us find peace in Christ?

_____

_____

_____

_____

_____

Catechism: 2828–2830

In the Sermon on the Mount, Jesus insists on the filial trust that cooperates with our Father's providence (Matthew 6:25–34). He is not inviting us to idleness, but wants to relieve us from nagging worry and preoccupation. Such is the filial surrender of the children of God. (2830)

1. When teaching us not to worry, Jesus promised that if we seek first his kingdom, all things will be given to us (Matthew 6:33). Why should a confidence that we are doing the will of God relieve us of worry and anxiety?

_____

_____

_____

_____

_____

2. Why is surrender to our Father important? Why do you think so many people find it difficult to surrender their problems to the Lord?

_____

_____

_____

_____

3. How can preoccupation with our own troubles prevent us from reaching out to others in need?

_____

_____

_____

_____

For Further Reflection and Discussion:

1. What kinds of things do you worry about? Why do they cause you to worry?

_____

_____

_____

_____

2. What are the consequences of worry and anxiety on the quality of your life and your relationships with others?

_____

_____

_____

_____

_____

3. If we allow worry to consume us, what does that say about our relationship with the Lord?

_____

_____

_____

_____

_____

4. Share any victories you have experienced over worry or anxiety in your life. Were there any Scripture verses you relied on to help you? Make a list of some Scripture verses that you can memorize and pray when you realize you are worrying about something. (You can find expressions of trust in the Lord in many of the psalms.)

_____

_____

_____

_____

_____

Developing a Servant's Heart 14

*J*esus was the ultimate servant. He served each one of us to the point of laying down his life for us. "For the Son of Man came not be served but to serve, and to give his life as a ransom for many" (Mark 10:45). As Christians, we are also called to be servants. But to be an effective servant, we need to have the heart of a servant. That often means a willingness to "die to self" out of love for our brothers and sisters, by putting aside our own needs and desires for the needs of others.

After years of living in another state, Mindy's aging parents had moved into a retirement community nearby. Mindy and her family were excited about being able to see her parents more often, but Mindy also didn't realize how often they would need her help. She accompanied them to doctors' appointments and paid their bills. Her husband helped them with work around their home. There were many times when Mindy felt burdened by the additional responsibilities, and sometimes she felt resentful that her other siblings, who lived farther away, did not pitch in to help her.

One day Mindy was complaining to her friend Ellen about the situation. Ellen, who also cared for her parents, listened intently, and agreed that that it could be quite burdensome. "If I keep in mind that I am serving my parents out of love, then I don't feel resentful when they need me," Ellen said. Mindy was struck by this thought. Perhaps if she viewed everything she did as an act of love and service—rather than as an intrusion and imposition on her time—she might feel differently. As Mindy took on this attitude, she was able to serve her parents, family, and friends cheerfully. Over time, she was even grateful that God was giving her many opportunities to love others by serving them.

Scripture: John 13:3–15

[3]Jesus, knowing that the Father had given all things into his hands, and that he had come from God and was going to God, [4]got up from the table, took off his outer robe, and tied a towel around himself. [5]Then he poured water into a basin and began to wash the disciples' feet and to wipe them with the towel that was tied around him. [6]He came to Simon Peter, who said to him, "Lord, are you going to wash my feet?" [7]Jesus answered, "You do not know now what I am doing, but later you will understand." [8]Peter said to him, "You will never wash my feet." Jesus answered, "Unless I wash you, you have no share with me." [9]Simon Peter said to him, "Lord, not my feet only but also my hands and my head!" [10]Jesus said to him, "One who has bathed does not need to wash, except for the feet, but is entirely clean. And you are clean, though not all of you." [11]For he knew who was to betray him; for this reason he said, "Not all of you are clean."

[12]After he had washed their feet, had put on his robe, and had returned to the table, he said to them, "Do you know what I have done to you? [13]You call me Teacher and Lord—and you are right, for that is what I am. [14]So if I, your Lord and Teacher, have washed your feet, you also ought to wash one another's feet. [15]For I have set you an example, that you also should do as I have done to you."

1. How could Jesus fill the dual roles of master and servant at the same time? Why are these roles in many cases one and the same?

_____

_____

_____

_____

_____

2. Washing the feet of a guest was a job usually reserved for the lowliest of servants, which is why Peter reacted so violently at first to Jesus' intention to wash his own feet. What made him change his mind? Do you think the disciples understood the symbolism of Jesus' action at the time?

_____

_____

_____

_____

_____

3. How does this passage inspire you to serve? How does it change your feelings about being served?

_____

_____

_____

_____

_____

Catechism: 783, 786, 2013

The People of God fulfills its royal dignity by a life in keeping with its vocation to serve with Christ. (786)

"The faithful should use the strength dealt out to them by Christ's gift, so that . . . doing the will of the Father in everything, they may whole-heartedly devote themselves to the glory of God and to the service of their neighbor"(*Lumen gentium* 40 § 2). (2013)

1. Although Jesus is King and Lord of the universe, he came "not to be served but to serve." In what practical ways are you being called to serve others?

_____

_____

_____

_____

_____

2. As you contemplate Jesus' service to humanity, which culminated in his laying down his life, do you ever fear the cost of serving? If so, how can you overcome those fears?

_____

_____

_____

_____

_____

3. Why do you think service to our neighbor glorifies God? Think of someone you know with a servant's heart. How is our Christian witness strengthened by our attitude of service?

_____

_____

_____

_____

_____

For Further Reflection and Discussion:

1. Make a list of all the ways you served others today. Are you surprised by how often you serve? Why or why not?

_____

_____

_____

_____

_____

2. Why is it especially important that people in authority—especially parents—have a servant's heart? What happens when this attitude is missing?

_____

_____

_____

_____

_____

3. What obstacles do you face in developing a servant's heart? (Some common obstacles: pride, self-pity, haughtiness, laziness, or resentment.) What areas of service are particularly difficult for you?

_____

_____

_____

_____

_____

4. Share a time when you were served by others. How did it make you feel? Why do you think we are sometimes reluctant to let others serve us?

_____

_____

_____

_____

_____

Finding 15 Balance

Have you ever felt overwhelmed—with so much to do that you just don't know where to begin? That's an all-too-familiar feeling these days as women stretch themselves at home, in the workplace, and in their parishes. Unfortunately, in our achievement- and performance-oriented society, we often fail to acknowledge the need that God has placed in us for rest and recreation. Because we are beloved daughters of our Father, we need to set before him all that we have to do, and try to discern *his* priorities for our lives.

Tracy had just begun a new part-time nursing job after ten years of being a stay-at-home mom. However, she still wanted to be involved in her parish and at her kids' school, so she tried juggling all of her responsibilities at once. Unfortunately, she felt as if she was always on the move and always behind on what needed to be done. Her mornings started early, so she hadn't been spending much time in prayer. She was always tired, and she knew she had been snapping at her husband and kids.

Late one afternoon after a long day at work, Tracy walked into her house and collapsed on the couch. The day was far from over—her daughter needed help with her homework, she had to shuttle her son to soccer practice, and she had a church meeting that evening. When Tracy realized all she had to do and how tired she felt, she burst into tears.

Tracy knew she needed to sit down and talk to the Lord. She retreated to her bedroom, and began to pray that he would help her reorder her life. She needed to put all that she did before her Father, and let him direct her to what was most important. Above all, she needed to begin and end her days in prayer so that she would have the strength and grace to be a good wife, mother, nurse, and friend.

Scripture: Luke 10:38–42

[38]Now as they went on their way, he entered a certain village, where a woman named Martha welcomed him into her home. [39]She had a sister named Mary, who sat at the Lord's feet and listened to what he was saying. [40]But Martha was distracted by her many tasks; so she came to him and asked, "Lord, do you not care that my sister has left me to do all the work by myself? Tell her then to help me." [41]But the Lord answered her, "Martha, Martha, you are worried and distracted by many things; [42]there is need of only one thing. Mary has chosen the better part, which will not be taken away from her."

1. St. Luke describes Martha as "distracted by her many tasks" (10:40). What would have happened if Martha had put aside her chores to sit at Jesus' feet with her sister?

_____

_____

_____

_____

_____

2. Based on this passage, what are the risks of diving into active service without first seeking the Lord in prayer? If you are unable to start each day with prayer, what changes could you make that would allow you to do so?

_____

_____

_____

_____

_____

_____

3. Many women are so busy with what needs to get done that they have difficulty being able to calm themselves enough to sit in the Lord's presence. If you have this problem, how can Jesus' words in this passage help you?

_____

_____

_____

_____

_____

Catechism: 2184–2185

Just as God "rested on the seventh day from all his work which he had done" (Genesis 2:2), human life has a rhythm of work and rest. The institution of the Lord's Day helps everyone enjoy adequate rest and leisure to cultivate their familial, cultural, social, and religious lives. (2184)

1. Why is it important to respect the needs God placed in us for both work and rest? If you are tempted to ignore your need for rest and leisure, why do you think this is the case?

_____

_____

_____

_____

_____

_____

2. How do you and your family observe the Lord's Day? If you use Sundays as just another day to catch up on chores, what changes could you and your family make?

_____

_____

_____

_____

_____

3. What family activities or events do you find most relaxing? Which promote the best time for relating to one another? As a family, what can you do to increase these times?

_____

_____

_____

_____

_____

For Further Reflection and Discussion :

1. Imagine yourself in a conversation with the Lord about how you spend your time. In which areas do you think he would tell you to cut back? Where do you think he would want you to spend more time?

_____

_____

_____

_____

_____

2. Think about whether your expectations for yourself, your family, your home, and your career are realistic. Are these expectations coming from you, from the culture in which you live, or from God? What expectations might need to change?

_____

_____

_____

_____

3. If you take on more volunteer activities than you should, what causes you to do so? Of those volunteer efforts in which you are currently involved, which are those you are sure the Lord is calling you to do and which are those you do for other reasons?

_____

_____

_____

4. How often do you take time off to go away, either alone with your husband, or on a retreat or day of reflection? How has this refreshed you?

_____

_____

_____

_____

_____

The Storing 16 of Treasure

Our Father in heaven calls us, his beloved daughters, to spread the good news about Jesus and build his kingdom on earth. This means that we need to have the right attitude about money and possessions, even as we live in a materialistic society in which many people make idols of these things. Most of us are not called to give away all of our possessions and live in poverty, but we are called to be good stewards of what we own. Always we need to examine our hearts to make sure that we are not spending too much time and energy accumulating money and "things," and that we are using what God has given us to serve him and to further his purposes on earth. Above all, we cannot let our possessions possess us!

Kathy was proud of her tastefully decorated home, which she and her husband Mike had purchased two years ago. It was new, spacious, and located in an upscale neighborhood. Kathy and Mike were so excited about their new home that they had cut back on most of their volunteer activities so they could spend their free time painting, papering, and finding just the right furnishings. The mortgage was hefty, but they figured that their incomes would be growing in a few years. Then they could start to save for the future and contribute more to their parish.

One morning as they were about to leave for work, their son came into the living room screaming, "I smell smoke!" Kathy and Mike ran upstairs to find the hallway thick with smoke. They called 911, got everyone out of the house, and waited for the fire trucks to come. By the time they arrived, the second floor of their home was completely engulfed in flames. Their minds reeled as they thought of all the beautiful things they were losing. The fire was extinguished, but not before everything they owned had been destroyed by flames, smoke, or water.

Scripture: Matthew 6:19–21, 24

[19]"Do not store up for yourselves treasures on earth, where moth and rust consume and where thieves break in and steal; [20]but store up for yourselves treasures in heaven, where neither moth nor rust consumes and where thieves do not break in and steal. [21]For where your treasure is, there your heart will be also.

[24]"No one can serve two masters; for a slave will either hate the one and love the other, or be devoted to the one and despise the other. You cannot serve God and wealth."

1. Why do you think people are tempted to accumulate things that will not last? Why did Jesus warn his followers about the problem of accumulating material possessions?

_____

_____

_____

_____

2. What "heavenly" treasures are you storing up in your life? Why are these treasures more permanent than "earthly" treasures?

_____

_____

_____

_____

3. Why is it impossible to serve God and wealth at the same time?

_____

_____

_____

_____

_____

Catechism: 952, 2536, 2544–2547

"Everything the true Christian has is to be regarded as a good possessed in common with everyone else. All Christians should be ready and eager to come to the help of the needy . . . and of their neighbors in want" (*Roman Catechism*, I, 10, 27). A Christian is a steward of the Lord's goods. (952)

Jesus enjoins his disciples to prefer him to everything and everyone. . . . The precept of detachment from riches is obligatory for entrance into the Kingdom of heaven. (2544)

1. How does your attitude about wealth affect your ability to balance your time and energy between your family, your job, and your spiritual life?

_____

_____

_____

_____

_____

2. What events and experiences in your life helped to form your values about material possessions? Which experiences were positive and which were negative?

_____

_____

_____

_____

_____

3. How often do you rely on shopping and buying new things to give you an emotional lift? Make a list of other activities that would give you a similar lift but do not involve money.

_____

_____

_____

_____

For Further Reflection and Discussion:

1. Many women desire trendy or expensive things because they want to appear significant in the eyes of others, even when they can't afford them. How often is this a motivation for you? How can a closer relationship with God fulfill the need for significance?

_____

_____

_____

_____

_____

2. Sometimes we can experience discontent because we desire more money or possessions than we have. What are some practical ways to battle discontent?

_____

_____

_____

_____

_____

3. Why is it important to view everything you own as a gift from God? How could a fuller awareness of this truth change your behavior?

_____

_____

_____

_____

_____

4. In what ways can you use your treasure (your home, your possessions, your money) to provide for the needs of others?

_____

_____

_____

_____

_____

About the Authors

Patricia Mitchell has served as editor of The Word Among Us Press since 1999. Before that, she was a staff writer for *The Word Among Us* magazine. She is the author of *I Have Called You by Name: The Stories of 16 Saints and Christian Heroes*, and editor of *Wisdom from Pope John Paul II*, *Wisdom from Dorothy Day*, and *A Year of Celebration: Experiencing God in the Feast Days of the Church*. Patty and her husband John have four children and live in Virginia.

Bill Bawden is a permanent deacon who serves as pastoral associate at St. John's Catholic Church in Edmond, Oklahoma. Author of *Signposts: How To Be a Catholic Man in the World Today*, he is cofounder of the Oklahoma Fellowship of Catholic Men and a popular speaker at Catholic men's conferences. Bill and his wife Sylvia have three children and three grandchildren and live in Edmond, Oklahoma.